DISCOVERING YOU

GIRL *got* FAITH

DISCOVERING YOU

First published in Great Britain in 2021

Society for Promoting Christian Knowledge
36 Causton Street
London SW1P 4ST
www.spck.org.uk

Photographs © Abbie Young, YouVersion, Alexandra Glass, Olivia Ema,
Unsplash, Letita Wright, Naomi Scott, Ashley John-Baptiste, Emma Borquaye,
Yasmin Elizabeth, Zachary Chick, Riccardo Castano - ISSTUDIO, Bel Litchfield, Bella Thomas.

British Library Cataloguing-in-Publication Data
A catalogue record for this book is available from the British Library

ISBN 978-0-281-08510-1
eBook ISBN 978-0-281-08586-6

1 3 5 7 9 10 8 6 4 2

Typeset by Emily Langford, SPCK
First Printed and bound in Turkey by Imago Publishing Limited

eBook by Nord Compo

Produced on paper from sustainable forests

This book is a beautiful accompaniment for any girl seeking to live an empowered life with Jesus at the centre.
Rachel Gardner, Director of National Work, Youthscape

I believe that this book will be a welcome breath of fresh air for young women around the world who are on a journey to understand who they are.

It's been a pleasure over the years to watch the ministry of Girl Got Faith grow from strength to strength. *Discovering You* is a go-to for every girl who is wondering who they are and why they are here.
Lily-Jo, Founder of The Lily-Jo Project

Practical, honest, life-giving, fun, relatable, encouraging, full of truth, real talk, real stories and real gals. Big fan of the activities too, I'm a sucker for activities. Ohhhh one more thing, I LOVE Emma's notes throughout, feels like an older sister checking in to see how you're taking it all in! I hope you love it just as much as I did - so brilliant!
Elle Limebear, Worship leader and songwriter

What I love about this book and the author Emma is that Emma is so passionate about us knowing who we are in God. When we know who we are in God, we are limitless.
Michelle Williams, Music artist and mental health advocate

Dear reader,

may you discover the powerful truth of who you are and all that you have been created for.

You've got this!

Emma

Hey Girl

This book belongs to

Contents

Starting with you

Let's start with you.

This might be a surprising place to begin if we are looking at building a life centred on God, but the amazing thing about a life of faith is that God always meets us where we are.

It's important for us to acknowledge where we are coming from so that we can get on the path to where we want to end up.

In this section, we are going to begin by exploring what makes you who you are. From the importance and impact of identity to hearing from actress Letitia Wright about how everything changed when she discovered her identity in God, and what life looks like when you allow your faith to take centre stage. I hope that these pages encourage you that you are important because you are important to God.

I want to remind you that this book is *yours.* You can treat it like a diary if you want; you don't need to show anyone, and you can be completely honest here. When we can be raw and real with ourselves, it allows room for a whole lot of healthy stuff to begin to grow within us.

So, let's go!

Identity

Identities help us find our place in the world.

The dictionary defines 'identity' as 'the fact of being who you are', but that's not super helpful, is it?

Let's look at it this way: imagine you are in a room of people that you have never met. How would you introduce yourself?

We tend to follow the pattern of sharing our name, what we do, where we live, maybe even how old we are. And without thinking about it too much, we can start to take these things on as our identity. These are all elements of your life, but they don't make you who you are.

Maybe you have had experiences in life that have started to shape who you believe you are in a more negative way, such as unkind words from someone you love, or the way that you've been unfairly or wrongly treated. These things can be extremely hurtful, and we may need support to process and release some of these things that we have been made to believe about ourselves, but I want you to know that not a single one of them is powerful enough to give you your true identity.

You were created thoughtfully and intricately. God wouldn't leave it up to temporary things, sinful people, or society and its structures to define who you are. There is only one who has the authority to give you your identity, and that is God who created you. Therefore, if we were to rewrite the dictionary, we would define 'identity' as 'who God created you to be'.

As you turn the page, you are about to discover your true identity — one that is unchanging, full of truth and cannot be taken away from you. Let these words be as true to you as your own name. They are a banner over you — your title, your confidence, and your value.

Identity in Christ

Child of God

Reconciled

Not condemned

Justified

Righteous

Ambassador

Forgiven

Loved

Temple

Blameless

Salt

Light

Chosen

Heir

Included

Saint

Sanctified

Royalty

Created

Purposeful

Rescued

Complete

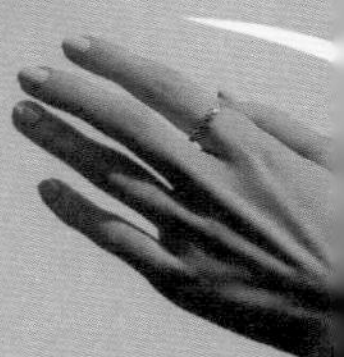

Fearless

Adopted

Free

Established

Anointed

Witness

A citizen of
heaven

Seated with
Christ

God's
workmanship

Overcomer

Strengthened
through Christ

A note from Emma

Hey girls,

Can I take a moment to be really honest with you guys?

The truth is, once I began writing the words scattered over the previous page declaring your identity in God, I had to stop because I didn't actually believe them for myself. How could I tell you to receive these words and declare them as a banner over you while still doubting that they were true for me?

I took a moment to reflect on why I was finding this God-given identity so difficult to believe.

I think sometimes we hear these words so much in church or from kind people in our lives that we think 'you're just saying that to be nice.' Then, our mind goes into overdrive as we begin guessing all the things that person must *really* think of us.

I have grown up in church my whole life, and even though I wholeheartedly believe the Bible is the true word of God, when it comes to what it says about me, I still don't always take it at its word. I regularly struggle with self-doubt, but as I found myself

listing out these words to share with you, I knew I didn't want to stay in that place of never really receiving my true identity.
I read somewhere recently that around 90 per cent of your whole brain function is subconscious, meaning that there is only ten per cent that is actually conscious and intentional. I had a revelation in this moment that it is our subconscious mind that ends up dictating the majority of how we see ourselves, but if we want to think differently, we need to be intentional with the ten per cent of consciousness we have.

So, to put this into practice, I began speaking out these words and reading them in the same way I would read my very own name. I would also take time to think about each word individually and conclude how and why it is true, rather than rushing on to the next word.

The reason I'm telling you this is because I want to encourage you that if you are struggling to accept these names over you, you're not alone. Believing them can be a battle, especially as we constantly have other things in our lives telling us something different and throwing doubt into the mix. But we can choose to be intentional and use that ten per cent of our brain to have a greater influence over the 90 per cent that is subconscious. Begin by choosing just one word from the 'Identity in Christ' page today and telling that ten per cent of your brain that it's 100 per cent true.

love,
Emma x

Made in God's image

The concept of being made in God's image can be confusing because we may interpret this as meaning we physically look like God, the same way you might resemble one of your family members. But we all look different, so how can we possibly all be made in God's image?

John Piper is a theologian who explains it simply like this: 'Images are created to image. If you create an image, if you make a sculpture of someone, you do it to display something about that someone. You put it in the square in the middle of town, and you want people to look at it, notice it, think about that person, think something about them — that they were noble or strong or wise or courageous or something. Now what would it mean if you created seven billion statues of yourself and put them all over the world? It would mean you would want people to notice you. God created us in his image so that we would display or reflect or communicate who he is, how great he is, and what he is like.'

Being made in God's image means that every single aspect of your created being was made with the intention to reflect something of the image of God himself. That even includes your physical body. The skin you are in, your body shape, your hair texture, your height, your eyes. You were made entirely in the image of God, and God makes no mistakes, so there is no mistake in you, Daughter of the Most High King.

The world we live in has instead become fixated with the mirror reflection of ourselves. We are told to change what we see in the mirror until we represent the standard of 'beauty' that society has set for us. But the truth is, this is completely unattainable. We were never created to all look the same, and there is no one appearance that is 'most beautiful'.

Depending on where you live and what era you were born into, the standard of beauty will be very different. It constantly changes and evolves over time, and ultimately there will be no winner in the beauty pageant of life. There is so much to be undone here as this 'view of self' is deeply rooted in our humanity, so we really are just skimming the surface, but we can start with a very simple prayer.

Lord,

Please help me to see myself the way that you see me. Help me to understand that I am created in your image and allow that to produce a gratitude and a love for every aspect of my physical body, even when the world is telling me that I need to change. Help me to truly love who you have created me to be.

Amen

Your body isn't bad

We couldn't talk about image without addressing
body image, so we asked our wonderful friend
Cheryl Fagan to share a special guest feature that will
help us navigate the way we see ourselves, including
some practical body-love tips to get us started
on our self-love journey.

Cheryl Fagan is a Sex Educator and the Founder of On Top, with an academic background in Psychology and Sexual & Reproductive Health.

In 2018, Cheryl published *On Top: Your Personal Study Guide to Holistic Sexuality* — an educational guide for teenagers and community groups.

There are countless studies showing how young people are not happy with their bodies. Research from the US Department of Health and Human Services shows that body image and self-esteem go hand in hand — young people with poor self-image tend to get involved in 'harmful' situations, i.e. substance abuse, unsafe friendships, rushing into sex, self-harm.

The media tells us how our bodies should look. Unfortunately, the message it gives is an unrealistic standard for both boys and girls to act and behave in a certain way.

Do you ever wonder why the media has such influence and impact on the way we view ourselves? The media is clever; instead of speaking to our intellect, they speak to our emotions. By speaking into people's desires and using fear tactics, they have the power to make us believe we need a particular product to be accepted, pretty, valuable, cool, etc. However, there is hope because the Bible actually talks about our image, too! This foundational truth can shape the way we view ourselves. Let's see what it says.

In Genesis 1.26–27, God spoke: 'Let us make human beings in our image, make them reflecting our nature ... God created human beings; he created them godlike, reflecting God's nature. He created them male and female.' (MSG)

Do you get what this actually means? The Creator of the earth made you and me like him! The amazing attributes of a man are actually a direct reflection of God, and the attributes of a woman reflect another side of him, which is why we are equal. Like God, you are creative, you are intelligent, you are spiritual, you are a communicator, you have a sense of morality and you have a purpose.

I realize this can sound cliché or a bit cheesy, but it's a truth in the Bible that is so often misunderstood. Psalm 139.13–16 (MSG) says,

> Oh yes, you shaped me first inside, then out; you formed me in my mother's womb. I thank you, High God—you're breathtaking! Body and soul, I am marvelously made! I worship in adoration— what a creation! You know me inside and out, you know every bone in my body; You know exactly how I was made, bit by bit, how I was sculpted from nothing into something. Like an open book, you watched me grow from conception to birth; all the stages of my life were spread out before you. The days of my life all prepared before I'd even lived one day.

It's my belief that our life stories don't start at conception. Life begins before our parents even met. God knew you. He knew you then, and he knows you now. He cares about you. He loves you regardless of your upbringing or the choices you've made. He has a plan just for you.

Body-love tips

*Taking care of our bodies helps us to love our bodies.
When it comes to feeling comfortable in your skin and
building a healthier relationship with your body, there are
a few little tricks you can try to take care of yourself.*

01
Eat healthily

02
Give yourself oil massages

03
Use a dry body brush in long, pressured strokes to increase circulation

04
Don't rush taking care of your body (like when you moisturize)

05
List the things about your body that you are grateful for

What makes you happy?

Now that we understand a little more about what it means to be made in the image of God and that it involves every aspect of our created being, we can be confident that even our unique personalities are an expression of God. So whether you are introverted, extroverted, love marmite or hate it, you are exactly who God created you to be.

The same way the world tells us how we should look, it also tells us what we need to be happy. Maybe it's that we need to look like her, have their style, own this stuff or be loved by that man. Through all of these expectations, we can lose our sense of what truly makes us happy in our own unique, personal and perfectly designed way. To honour God's creative expression in us, let's get back in touch with what really makes us happy and embrace the uniqueness that our Creator has given us without worrying about what it might do to our social status.

We asked people from our online Girl Got Faith community to tell us the weird and wonderful things that makes them happy. Why don't you tick the ones that make you happy, and then add a few of your own if you want to.

Things That Make Us Happy

- Constant laughter
- Long conversations with my bestie over a cup of tea
- Singing and dancing
- Coffee and my devotional
- Exercising
- Melted Camembert and crusty white bread
- New socks
- The sound of the sea
- When the sunshine flickers through the curtains
- Comfortable friendships
- Being healthy
- Baking cupcakes
- Chicken nuggets
- Feeling content
- Food
- Listening to old records
- New music
- Singing along to Mamma Mia
- Feeling understood
- The sun on my skin
- Putting my pyjamas on
- The violin
- Seeing my friends laugh
- Books
- Laughing with my mum and sister
- Complimenting a stranger
- Dreaming of the future
- Being outside
- Knowing that those I love are safe
- Feeling loved
- A clean and organized house
- Catching up with my friends
- My family
- Travelling
- Getting ready slowly
- A cup of tea

- Journaling
- Dancing
- Singing worship songs
- Church
- Reading in bed with a hot chocolate
- Performing on stage
- Spontaneous adventures
- Floating on water
- Animals
- Giving gifts
- Cookie dough
- Baths
- Massages

- Being productive
- Guinea pigs
- My cat's big belly
- Knowing that God loves me
- Youth group
- Fresh bedsheets
- Watching funny videos
- Car journeys with my family
- Me time
- Shopping
- Pampering myself
- Playing the harp
- Chocolate
- Rainy days

- My dogs
- Watching TV after school
- Cake
- Ballet
- Calligraphy
- Oreo cookies
- Reminiscing with friends
- Seeing my mum
- Netflix and pizza
- Caring people
- Light through the window when you wake up
- Playing sport
- Shopping in the sales
- Clean shoes
- Crunchy leaves
- Waking up early
- Worship music
- Camping
- Art
- Acting
- Horse Riding
- Cooking videos
- Kittens
- Festivals
- Pretty flowers
- A good book
- Having a lie-in
- Sunset
- Puppies
- Popcorn
- Chocolate brownies
- Long walks
- The colour purple
- Daydreaming
- Freshly baked bread
- _____
- _____
- _____
- _____

But what about my weaknesses?

All of us were created perfectly in God's image, but what about the parts of us that feel a lot less than perfect? How we react in anger when someone hurts us; a jealousy that drives us; the selfishness that consumes us?

We were born into a world of sin, which means that throughout life our sinful nature can take hold of us — the Bible calls these things the fruits of our flesh. We are not called to love and accept the sinful parts of ourselves but instead to surrender ourselves to God and receive the Holy Spirit, who can transform us from the inside out, helping us to come back in step with who God really created us to be: image bearers of him.

The incredible thing is that the Holy Spirit alive in us turns even our weaknesses into a platform for the strength of God to be displayed through our lives.

We don't need to live in shame; God does not identify us by our weaknesses, but instead, when we receive his spirit, we get a new identity as overcomers! We become the recipients of the fruits of the spirit: *'But the fruit of the Spirit is love, joy, peace, patience, kindness, goodness, faithfulness, gentleness, self-control'* *(Galatians 5.22–23 ESV)*.

We don't need to fear our weaknesses, and we don't need to feel shame for our sins, but instead continually submit them to God and ask for the Holy Spirit to be alive in us every day.

Fearfully and wonderfully made 🖊

Make this flowchart personal to you by being bold and honest with
your answers. You'll discover that we are all wonderful in our own way!

The thing that *makes me wonderful* is ...

Something that makes *someone else wonderful* could be ...

I don't need to compete
or feel jealous because ...

God made me
with a purpose so I can be
confident that ...

And this makes me ...

*Fearfully
and
Wonderfully
Made*

An interview with

Letitia Wright

Letitia is a BAFTA-winning actress and the star of the
Marvel film *Black Panther*. She's had several roles
in British TV series and, by the age of 26, had even
started her own production company. She works hard and
achieves big, but it's her warmth and humility that leave
the greatest imprint every time she speaks.

We catch a moment to chat all things deep and meaningful, from overcoming depression to finding confidence in who God created her to be.

What was life like growing up for you?

I was born in Guyana, South America, and life back home was simple and very family-oriented, teaching me a lot about respect and acknowledgement of different people. When I moved to the UK around the age of seven, it felt kind of strange to me to not know your neighbours, to be in the confinements of your home with just your family.

When I started school, I just didn't fit in. I had a different accent from everyone, so I'd listen to how people say certain words and copy them — that's where the acting first started to step in.

When you were in your early 20s, that's when you found faith for yourself. How did that come about?

I spent my teenage years trying to find myself and my contentment in different things — in acting, in achieving, in accolades — but I just couldn't find it. I knew that something wasn't right.

Then, one by one, I started to see some of my friends from drama school become Christians. I was just like, something's going on here; why are they all running to Christ? Even so, I was adamant that it was not for me. That was until in 2015, when I found myself going through a very difficult time — one where you feel like you're in the darkness alone and nobody sees you. But then a friend called me to tell me that God had revealed to him that I wasn't happy and that I should try Jesus. 'No,' I told him. 'Jesus is a blonde-haired, blue-eyed guy who has nothing to do with me!' And he was like, 'I'm not talking about how he looks. I'm talking about his spirit and the fact that he will set you free.'

I came off the phone and prayed, 'Jesus, if you're real, prove it; I'm giving you a year.' Not long after, a friend invited me to church, and I said, 'okay yeah!' before thinking, *eww, wait, why did I say that?*

What was that experience of church like for you?

I went there and remember looking at the preacher and thinking, 'I'm not coming back.' But then, as we stood up to pray, I started to feel very light-headed, and I just fell.

Next thing I know, I felt these hands on me and people were praying for me. After that, I kept going to the church, asking questions and asking God to prove himself until I knew I had to make an exchange. I gave him all of my sin and the things that were painful in my life and made an exchange with him to get free. As soon as I got saved, I went through this whirlwind of looking at my life so far and could see that I didn't know who I was; wasn't operating in the fullness as a child of God.

I had placed my identity in so many things, but every time I tried to achieve that 'thing', it wasn't fulfilling. The more I got into the Word, the more I prayed, I started to realize my worth wasn't actually in acting; my worth wasn't in someone liking me. My worth was actually in the fact that God loves me and he set me free.

You speak openly about how prior to this, when your friend came to you, you were suffering with depression. How do you think we can take mental health really seriously without allowing it to become our identity?

For me, it's about your mind being reformed and renewed. With my depression, I noticed that it wasn't the natural way for me to be. Being in a dark room and having suicidal thoughts was not right, and when Jesus projected the truth of who I am in him, I saw that my depression wasn't who I truly am. It needed to go, whether through therapy,

Jesus or both. I believe in Jesus and therapy! Jesus and talking to people and meeting with friends. People ask why I never stop talking about Jesus, but he saved me and set my mind free, so if someone else feels like they don't deserve that or like they won't ever get it, I have to tell them that that's not true.

I love how the Bible speaks about the fruits of the Holy Spirit. It promotes God's natural way of being for us: peace, love, happiness, joy, gentleness, patience. When I see young people go through what I've been through, I try to tell them about these things and say, let's talk, let's get some help so you can be better at recognizing when those thoughts, anxieties and worries come.

You're really vocal about your faith. Has anyone ever prejudged you and then they meet you and say something like 'ah you're cool for a Christian!'?

I haven't actually experienced that — or at least they haven't told me — but I have found that people often have questions. I remember, when filming *Death on the Nile*, I was eating a burger and chips in this hotel in the middle of nowhere, and Dawn French asked, 'Can I sit with you?' Later, she said, 'I've seen you talk about Jesus; I really love it. I can see it's really helped you and that you're genuine about what you say.' I've actually also had loads of moments where people ask me to pray for them.

Do you feel like your faith and even your identity in Christ helps you be more confident in your work?

Definitely. Before Christ, it was all on me. All on my shoulders. I was so worried about what people thought of me. I was depending on my own strength to cultivate this identity that I felt was beneficial for me to give out to the world and I would always be hard on myself. I would go back and analyze films and interviews I had done, thinking, 'Why did you pull that face? Why did you say that? You need to be more like this or dress more like that.' The second I came into Christ, it was so refreshing. I decided to quit acting. I was like, I'm not doing this anymore, because I've found a treasure that's so good that I don't want to mess it up. I felt God was like, 'yeah cool', and I quit some jobs that I had lined up to just seek Jesus.

In those four or five months of seeking Jesus, I started to see my worth in him and how much I was loved by him. I spent hours and hours each day praying and reading the word, and my mind just shifted into his idea and affirmation of who I am. As I was doing that, it was like God was plotting to bring acting back into my life again, but this time from the standpoint of being a vessel for him. If a project comes my way, I now ask, 'God, what's your will?' I'm in a partnership with him.

Considering now your view of work being different — how do you define success?

I really think success is being true to what God has placed in your heart. Success is partnering up with God and seeing it happen, whatever that is. Success for me is also not going against your morals and not compromising. I now try to bring everything to his feet, saying, 'God, I do acting. You bring characters for me to play. Is this still your will for me? Did heaven give the go-ahead?' I think a daily checking-in of 'am I still on the right path?' is important, and that is success in my eyes.

Do you feel like reading the Bible is when you feel the closest to God?

It varies. Some days I don't want to read the Bible, but I'll listen instead. Sometimes walking and praying feels good, and others, just being in my room and praying feels better. Sometimes I just want to worship, or be silent, or pray in the spirit until something shifts. However the Holy Spirit moves. What I have been

teaching myself now is that even if I don't feel like reading my Bible, I should still read it because I'll always get something out of it.
Sometimes I'll be reading, thinking, 'omg, I'm not taking anything in and I'm so bored, I'm thinking about cereal...' And then I close it, and someone says something, and I'm like, 'Dang, I read about that today!' I'm not perfect at it, but when I do get into it, though, it's like, 'OK, Tish, man, what have you been doing? This is so good!'

So now, after everything you have been through and the journey you are on, who is Letitia? How would your family describe you?

That's so hard. I guess they would say I'm just a young girl who's very ambitious, loves God and is trying to make a positive impact on the world with what she has been given in terms of her talent and who she is as a person.

If you imagine an average teenage girl today, with all the pressures of social media, TV, friends, school and whatever the world is trying to define her with, what would you want to tell her about her identity in Christ?

One of my little sisters is about to be 13, and I would just say, you don't have to figure everything out right now; just enjoy discovering who God made you to be. Sometimes that takes a little bit of time, and that's OK. So as long as you're close to God and you try every day just to find out more about him, he will reveal more about yourself to you in the process.

It's a journey, and you don't have to rush ahead to figure it all out as they claim that you need to; just enjoy that process of loving you and loving God.

Gideon's story

The trajectory of our life hinges on if we believe we are who God says we are and we can do what God says we can do. Don't believe me? Let's look at Gideon's story.

In the book of Judges, we read how Gideon was called upon by God to save the Israelites from the Midianites who were causing them a lot of grief and poverty. Gideon was minding his own business, harvesting wheat and hiding from the Midianites when an Angel of the Lord appeared to him. *'The Lord is with you, mighty warrior'* *(Judges 6.12 NIV)*.

The Angel is identifying Gideon as a mighty warrior — pretty cool. Gideon responds with "Pardon me?" as you would, and after the Angel of the Lord explains to Gideon what he is being called to do, Gideon seriously doubts his ability and thinks maybe it's a case of mistaken identity. 'How can I save Israel? My clan is the weakest in Manasseh, and I am the least in my family' (Judges 6:15 NIV).

Let's pause.

How did Gideon come to believe that his clan was the weakest, and who told him he was the least in his family?

This is a real man, who would have experienced real things the same way we do today. So, maybe it was a passing comment from his parent that made him feel like he wasn't as good as his siblings, or maybe it was humiliation from a so-called friend that made him believe he was from a weak family, but what we know is that Gideon has taken these titles of weakest and least and made them a part of his identity. But God has come to re-address him, to remind him of who he is, to remind him of his true identity.

In this short exchange, Gideon is encouraged that God will be with him in the mission, so he accepts and goes on to have one of the most incredible victory stories in the Bible — defeating an army of thousands with just 300 men.

When God worked with Gideon on his identity, he went from weakest and least to being remembered as one of the most courageous, wisest and faith-filled judges that there ever was over Israel. Not only did God work to change the course of Gideon's life, through him he also changed the course of a whole nation!

Don't underestimate the power that can come from you getting a handle on your identity. There are people who are counting on you, without even knowing it, to rise up and be all who God has called you to be.

Letter to a friend

You know your greatest fears, your biggest doubts and your most exciting dreams. If your best friend confided all of his or hers to you, how would you encourage that friend?

Write a letter to yourself from that perspective, encouraging and affirming yourself, calling out the lies behind your fears and building your confidence to pursue your dreams. The challenge is to find at least one Bible verse to include in the letter.

Facemask recipe

Self-care doesn't have to be complicated or expensive, particularly
when it comes to taking care of your skin! DIY face masks are great fun
to make, inexpensive and you can personalize them to suit your skin's
needs. Here's a fun guide for a really easy face mask that you can make
with your friends (or just when you feel like pampering yourself).

**Exfoliating and nourishing mask
(great for acne/hormonal breakouts)**

Ingredients

Avocado
The fatty acids in avocado nourish
and soften the surface of the skin.

Oatmeal
Pieces of oatmeal help to exfoliate
the skin and remove dead skin cells.
Oatmeal can also help to soak up
excess oil (great for oily skin types).

Honey
An added boost of hydration and
great for hormonal breakouts.

Method

Mash a (very ripe) avocado in a bowl
with the back of a fork until smooth.

Add 1 tablespoon of oatmeal into the
bowl and stir (add extra oatmeal for
more intense exfoliation).

Add 2 teaspoons of runny honey
(or more, if you added extra oatmeal)
into the mixture and stir until
everything is combined.

This recipe was brought to you by
Beauty Therapist, Samantha Kate, from Milk + Honey Wellbeing.

Application

Start by thoroughly cleansing your skin to remove any makeup or excess oil from the day. By removing the surface layer of makeup and oil, the ingredients in your face masks can work much harder and you will see the benefits much quicker!

Use your mask straight away and leave on for 10–15 minutes while you relax, watch a film and enjoy some snacks. Rub the mask into the skin to exfoliate, then remove with warm water and a flannel.

Things to note

DIY masks are great for having fun together and experimenting. If you are making masks with fresh, natural ingredients, just remember that they don't keep, so make enough for single use and make a new batch each time. If you are allergic to any of the listed ingredients, then don't apply to the skin. Consult a doctor if you are currently taking any skin medication or other medications which may be affected by the listed ingredients. If you do have any adverse reactions to any of the masks, then rinse immediately and consult a doctor.

The true you

If you're a more visual person, this activity will be perfect for you to get a true picture of who you are in Christ.

01   **Stick a picture of yourself in the middle of the page.**

02   **Look up the Bible verses below:**

      Psalm 139.14   Romans 8.37

      Jeremiah 1.5   John 3.16

      Isaiah 43.4   Ephesians 2.10

03   **In the spaces around your picture write the key word from each verse that relates to your identity.**

04   **You should end up with a wonderful bunch of words that share the truth of who you are!**

Your
photo
here

Contents

All about God

When you picture God, what do you imagine? Is he like a floating creature in the sky, or someone sitting on a throne beyond the clouds and just peering down at us on earth? How does the image you have of God affect how you relate to him and, more importantly, how you imagine he relates to you?

It's important that we reflect on these things because often it's these seemingly simple questions like 'who is God?' that we stumble over the most, sometimes realizing that we've never really discovered the answer for ourselves. If we truly want to live a life of faith, we should want to find out more about who we are living for; we can guarantee you won't be disappointed.

So, as we explore more of who God is over the next few pages, remember to be just as honest as you were in the last section. How you think and feel is valid, and God can *totally* handle it.

Who is God?

Naturally, the words we use to describe God will form our image of him, and that image will be based on our earthly experiences. For instance, you may hear that God is a king, or royalty, so you think about the royal family – they live in their castles, very separate from normal society, and you may think that they wouldn't really relate to you because their life would be so different from yours. Or maybe you hear about God as an authority, so you think about someone you know in authority – like a head teacher and how sometimes that teacher is harsh and strict or just very busy so doesn't have much time to spend with individual students unless they are in trouble. Or maybe it's that you've heard about God as a father, and your own earthly father hasn't been there for you the way that he should, or he has disappointed you and let you down.

These earthly comparisons can be helpful in our understanding of someone that we cannot see, but they can also be distracting when we try and grasp God's nature on a completely realistic level. Because the truth is, God is above all things – he actually is beyond what we could ever even imagine or have ever experienced. The Bible tells stories of people who saw glimpses of God and fell flat on their faces because of how majestic, glorious and powerful even the image of him is! So, we are going to look at a whole range of words that the Bible uses to describe God, and you'll get an idea of the fullness of who he is. He is in the valley and the mountaintop, the whisper and the wind.

Through the Holy Spirit as our helper, we can ask for an understanding that enables us to relate to God in a new way, knowing that when we speak to him, he hears us, he cares and he loves us with the fullness of who he is.

God the Father

by Ashley John-Baptiste

Ashley John-Baptiste spent most of his childhood in the UK care system and first entered the public eye as a member of a boy band that made it to the X Factor live finals. He is now a journalist and TV presenter as well as being an advocate for care leavers and an ambassador of the Fostering Network charity.

"

I had already spent what seemed like a lifetime in the care system.
I was already shunted between a number of homes, with no idea of
who my dad was. We never met.

I was 13 on that Friday evening when I was shopping with my foster
mum. In the grocery store – surrounded by others – I spotted a man
lift up a little boy, who appeared to be his son. The boy laughed in
delight. The father went on to tickle him and play fight. For some reason,
I was significantly struck by this simple display of fatherly affection.

As I watched the boy laugh hysterically at being tickled by his father,
something broke down on the inside of me. I plummeted inside.
Why didn't I have a dad to play with? Why was I rejected and put into
care? A wave of questions and emotions whirled inside, but outwardly
I played it cool.

When we got home, I ran to my bedroom and wept on my bed.
The pain of rejection and being fatherless was just too much.

I had started going to church with my foster mum and heard that God
could be a father to the orphan. In that moment, on my bed, I cried out
to God. If he was real, if the gospel was true — well then, I wanted him to
be my Father.

In that moment of crying out, I felt the embrace of a Father for the first
time in my life. In my weakness and vulnerability, I was reassured that
my life was in my heavenly Father's hands. He most certainly had a good
future for me.

Now, as an adult and father to a little girl, I am living proof of the reality
of the Father's love.

Who is god?

Love

Almighty

Lord of Hosts

Heaven's King

Ever true

Everlasting

Over all things

All powerful

All Knowing	Deliverer
Most high	Faithful
King of Kings	The vine
Gracious	Compassionate
Merciful	Forgiving
God of Justice	Righteous
The rock	Father
Creator	Friend
Redeemer	Safe place
Comforter	Patient

More about God
Digging deeper

What were some of your favourite descriptive words of God on the previous page? Some of ours would definitely include friend, God of all things, and Father.

It is through these words and the many other infinite characteristics of God that we can understand more about who God is, how he relates to us and how we can relate to him. For example, when we think of him as friend, it encourages us that we can speak to him the same way we do our earthly friends; we can talk about anything and everything, and we can have so much fun together. There's always an adventure to be had, and every moment shared with our friends is better than experiencing it alone. That's how it is with God.

Or, when we dwell on the fact that he is God of all things, we are reminded just how powerful and beyond comprehension he really is. This means that when we pray, we can believe and trust that he truly can make a difference. He has the power to change things in an instant. We don't need to worry about him trying to sort a load of stuff out before he gets to our needs, or having too much to handle. He is the God of all things, so he is the God of all *our* things.

When we think of God as Father, we must remember he is a perfect Father. For those who have had a good experience of an earthly father, we may be able to recall how parents have an ability that is beyond what they could create themselves to love their children.

Good parents want the best for us, and even when it may seem like they are holding us back from something, they can see the bigger picture and ultimately it will result in things being so much better for us in the future.

Most importantly, when we begin to gain our own understanding of who God is, we can realize how weird it would be to just take someone's word for it without experiencing a personal relationship with him. God is a personal friend, so, like any other friend, we wouldn't just hear something about who he is and accept that; we would want to get to know our friend, do life with our friend, experience the highs and lows with our friend. It's a relationship that lasts for all of eternity, so it is one worth investing in.

Nothing can separate us

Have you ever been on social media, and you've discovered a new account; you're browsing through some of his or her posts, and you think, 'Ah this person is really cool,' so you go to click 'follow' and it says 'follow back' because that person is *already* following you. It's a nice feeling to know that he or she had already seen you and reached out to you, had already taken a step into the friendship before you had even realized.

That's what our relationship with God is like. Yes, you may have just heard all these wonderful words describing who he is, and you think, wow, he sounds like a great guy; I want to know him more! But you aren't reaching out to him and hoping he notices you, or hoping he wants a relationship with you in return. He *already* chose you. He's *already* seen you; he's *already* taken that first step into your relationship, so you can come with full confidence, knowing you are wanted, chosen and loved.

The central story of the Bible is God's love for his creation (that's us!) and how when he created humans, he was so pleased, and the first-ever humans, Adam and Eve, were at one with God in Eden – that means they were walking around, living life, and actual God was present with them. God had instructed them on how they should live; however, they were tempted by the devil in the form of a serpent, and that is when sin entered the world. From this moment, they could no longer be alongside God, walking around with him, because it would be against God's very nature as holy and pure. Kind of like how when you add squash to water, it's not water anymore; it's squash. God can't mix with anything that isn't completely holy because it would change who he is — you get it?

So this is where God's rescue mission for humanity begins. He needed a way for there to be relationship between him and his people (us!) again, and there are a couple of different methods that are seen in the Old Testament, like animal sacrifices, or holy places/temples that only certain people can step into, and even then, they only get a small glimpse of him. But then comes Jesus — God's very *own* son! Jesus was fully man, yet fully God, and he was sent to this earth to walk just like us and experience what we experience. He would become the ultimate sacrifice, taking on all of our sin, even our future sin, and dying the death that we should have died. Remember, though, this wasn't just some easy thing for Jesus to do, or for God to plan. This was a huge deal, a heartbreaking moment where God had to turn away from his very own son. We hear the words from Jesus as he took his last breath on the cross: 'My God, My God, why have you forsaken me?' (Matthew 27.46).

But there was a *plan*! There always is with God. It was every bit real and painful in that moment, but God knew he had to go through that if he wanted to ever have a real, personal relationship with us. The Bible tells us that when Jesus died, the veil of the temple, which was the earthly dwelling place of God's presence, was torn in two, from top to bottom, signifying that there was now direct access from God to humanity. No longer a need for animal sacrifices or holy places for only a few people to access; access was granted to all of us. Through Jesus, we had all been made holy, pure as water, and ready for perfect relationship with God.

Who shall separate us from
the love of Christ?

Shall trouble or hardship
or persecution or famine or
nakedness or danger or sword?

As it is written:
"For your sake we face death
all day long; we are considered
as sheep to be slaughtered."
No, in all these things we are
more than conquerors through
him who loved us.

For I am convinced that neither
death nor life, neither angels
nor demons, neither the present
nor the future, nor any powers,
neither height nor depth,
nor anything else in all creation,
will be able to separate us
from the love of God that is
in Christ Jesus our Lord.

Romans 8.35-39
NIV

Hey girl

I just wanted to jump in here quickly with a little note from me.
I want to share something that took me a while to understand,
something I wish I had known way earlier. It's about forgiveness
– specifically, knowing you are forgiven.

I became a Christian at the age of seven and got baptized when I
was 15. I loved going to church with my family, and by my late teens
and early 20s, I knew quite a few scriptures and I felt I had a good
understanding of what it meant to be a Christian. However,
there was one truth I could never fully accept: *that I was forgiven*.

I messed up a lot, sometimes making the same mistakes over
and over again. I would get so down about this and feel like I had
separated myself from God. I felt overcome with shame and felt
like I couldn't pray until I had fixed myself up. But the problem
was, I didn't even know how to fix myself up. Even when I made a
few promises – like, I will never do this again – I was still doing the
wrong thing because I was trying to be my own saviour.

I knew all about what Jesus had done on the cross and that he
already paid the price for my sins, but I couldn't seem to apply
that to me. I thought it applied to people when they first became
Christians. You know how people say 'taking off the old and putting
on the new'. I thought that clean, fresh slate was only available
at the point of salvation and from there, your slate was your
responsibility to keep as clean as possible by not messing up and
being as good as you can.

But that wasn't really the design of God's forgiveness for us.

The result of my lack of understanding that Jesus had died not only for my past sin but my future sin too meant that I spent far too long punishing myself and staying away from God out of shame rather than running to him.

Like it says in Romans, there is nothing that can separate us from the love of God.

God had forgiven me. I just hadn't forgiven myself.

If that's you today, start with the prayer on the next page...

I then encourage you to delve deeper into understanding forgiveness and grace, read books, study it, talk about it. It's an important aspect of our relationship with God, ourselves and others, and when we truly grasp it, everything can change, just like it's changing for me too.

love,
Emma x

Dear God

Thank you that I am forgiven.
Thank you for the sacrifice that was made
for me through Jesus so that I could live in
freedom and have a personal relationship
with you. I have felt ashamed of my
mistakes and unable to forgive myself,
but I understand now that forgiveness is not
something I can work to achieve, nor punish
myself to receive, but it is a gift I already have.
I am free and I am forgiven. Please help me
to accept this truth and walk in it. I thank you
that each day you have new grace for me –
today, and every day, I receive it.

Amen

love never gives up. love cares more for others than for self. love doesn't
ce itself on others, Isn't always "me first," Doesn't fly off the handle, Do
ure in the flowering of truth, Puts up with anything, Trusts God always,
gives up. love cares more for others than for self. love doesn't want what i
n others, Isn't always "me first," Doesn't fly off the handle, Doesn't keep
flowering of truth, Puts up with anything, Trusts God always, Always look
ove cares more for others than for self. love doesn't want what it doesn't
n't always "me first," Doesn't fly off the handle, Doesn't keep score of the
uth, Puts up with anything, Trusts God always, Always looks for the best,
r others than for self. love doesn't want what it doesn't have. love doesn't
rst," Doesn't fly off the handle, Doesn't keep score of the sins of others,
th anything, Trusts God always, Always looks for the best, Never looks bac
r self. love doesn't want what it doesn't have love doesn't strut, Doesn't
ly off the handle, Doesn't keep score of the sins of others, Doesn't revel w
Trusts God always, Always looks for the best Never looks back , But keeps
doesn't want what it doesn't have. love doesn't strut, Doesn't have a swelle
andle, Doesn't keep score of the sins of others, Doesn't revel when others
ways, Always looks for the best, Never looks back , But keeps going to the
hat it doesn't have. love doesn't strut, Doesn't have a swelled head, Does
eep score of the sins of others, Doesn't revel when others grovel, Takes ple
oks for the best, Never looks back , But keeps going to the end. love never
have. love doesn't strut, Doesn't have a swelled head, Doesn't force itself
he sins of others, Doesn't revel when others grovel, Takes pleasure in the
best, Never looks back , But keeps going to the end. love never gives up. lo
doesn't strut, Doesn't have a swelled head, Doesn't force itself on others,
hers, Doesn't revel when others grovel, Takes pleasure in the flowering of
oks back , But keeps going to the end. love never gives up. love cares mor
doesn't have a swelled head, Doesn't force itself on others, Isn't always "m
evel when others grovel, Takes pleasure in the flowering of truth, Puts up
keeps going to the end. love never gives up. love cares more for others

Relationships
with God
at the centre

Relationships are everywhere: on TV, social media, magazines, billboards, films, and in your family. But what we often don't get to see are relationships with God at the centre. What does it look like and how does it work? Does it mean praying together every day and the worship night at church being your date night?

We decided to let our Girl Got Faith audience be the interviewers this time, and here they put their best Christian relationship questions to our founder, Emma, and her husband, Isaac.

How did you meet?

Isaac: I met Emma through a mutual friend of ours called Ben Lindsay; he used to run a venue that I performed at and every year he'd ask me if I had a girl. Then one time he said, 'Look, I think I've got someone that you might like'. He showed me a picture of Emma and then did some research, asking her brother-in-law to ask her if she likes rap music and tall guys and all that kind of stuff. And then he got me her number, but obviously I didn't text her straight away because I didn't want to come across like I was desperate. But my phone was in my pocket while I was at a concert, and I called her by accident. We had an awkward exchange but we just started chatting from there for about a month, until one day she said, 'Are you not going to ask me out?' So I did, and we went to an Italian restaurant in London. And the rest, as they say, is history.

Emma: We were dating for three years; we got engaged, and then we got married in 2015. So we've now been married for five years, which has gone so quickly, and we had a son in September 2019.

"
I prayed
for you before
I knew you
"

How do you pray together as a couple, and did you do that from the beginning of your relationship or just when you got married?

Emma: We didn't really pray together when we were first dating.

Isaac: I prayed for you before I knew you.

Emma: Aww, well yeah, it's always good to pray for the person if you're not necessarily praying together yet. But it doesn't mean it's not a Christian relationship if you're not praying together from day one. For us now in marriage we have very individual prayer lives, and our own personal relationships with God, and I think that's important. But then I think we do definitely try and be more intentional about praying together. We're not great at it – there are a lot of couples that do it all the time; they pray together every day.

Do you ever praise and worship together?

Emma: Do you know what?, I don't think we really do. Since we've had church at home, there's been more opportunity to 'worship' together, but we don't have set times where we'll be like, 'OK, let's stand and worship.'

Isaac: I don't see worship as a set thing that you say you're going to do – sometimes I'll be in the shower and I'll be playing a Kirk Franklin song, and we'll both be singing along, you know. I mean, so in that sense, yeah, we vibe to the same kind of music.

Does the man have to be good at leadership to be able to be a leader in marriage?

Isaac: That's a good question. I think I thought a husband should, and often men can put that pressure on themselves. I know I do. And a lot of guys that I speak to think they're not ready for marriage, or they're not ready for a relationship because they don't feel like a strong leader. But I think along the way, I've learned that leadership is more about admitting that you haven't got it all together and giving control away. And when you trust God to equip you with the tools that you need to lead your household and you approach that with a level of humility, God just gives you a lot of grace. I also think your wife will see where your heart is and see that you're trying to make decisions that aren't for your own benefit but for the benefit of the family and because you feel like it is what God wants you to do. So, yeah, I think guys need to stop putting pressure on themselves to be the most amazing leader; often leadership is about admitting your weaknesses and trusting God to help you with his strength and his power.

How do the dynamics in your friendships change once you get married or are in a relationship?

Isaac: I think when you start a life with someone, that's your primary responsibility. But that doesn't mean that you have to live inside each other's pockets 24/7. I think for both of us, we make a real effort to have our primary lives together, but also have our own time where we go and catch up with our friends and just really strengthen that dynamic because over time you don't see your friends as much as you used to. So, it's important to have that quality time with them as well.

At the start of your relationship, how did you go about setting boundaries between each other?

Emma: I always remember after our first date, Isaac drove me home, and I didn't find out until about a year later that he was so offended because I just got out of the car and said, 'Thanks, bye!' without even giving him a hug.

Isaac: If I didn't get a kiss, I would have been alright. But you could have reached over and given me a little hug and said thanks.

How it started

How it's going

Emma: But hugs in the car are awkward anyway!

Isaac: In all honesty, I remember driving home and thinking, 'rah she didn't even hug me', but I kind of rate it because it meant I had to work and she respects boundaries and stuff. But back to the question, I guess ultimately, we see our relationship as obviously we love each other, but we want to do things God's way. I think at the start of our relationship, if I'm being completely honest, we were trying to see how close we could get to the line without doing anything wrong.

But really, there isn't an actual line set out. It's about respecting one another and respecting God. Trying to do things his way as much as you possibly can, and keeping your eyes fixed on him rather than all the things you're 'not allowed' to do. We weren't perfect, but we took every day as it came, and didn't allow shame to throw us off track but got back up and tried again to do things God's way.

How do you pursue your dreams and ambitions while you're married?

Emma: I think Isaac and I are both quite ambitious people, and we have busy lives. But I do think that one of the biggest blessings of Christian marriage for me has actually been how Isaac has encouraged me in my dreams. I don't think he's ever been intimidated, and he's never told me to settle down or dampen my dreams. He's always been like, 'how can we make this happen?' And pushed me towards doing what God has called me to do. And I really value that in a partner. That is something that has really helped to shape my life and helped me to achieve things that I am really proud of.

Isaac: Yeah, if you try and get your partner to shine a bit less, it doesn't mean you're going to shine any more. But if you encourage each other to shine more, it's just a sick thing for the whole family.
Emma is my wife and the mother to my child which is a huge blessing, but that's not the only reason why God created her. That's not the only reason for being on this Earth. God's given her a purpose and potential, and I want to be able to stand in front of God and say I helped out on that journey. I helped her become what God wanted her to be, and I'm sure she'd want to say the same. So, yeah, I think you've got to encourage each other to be the best that you can be, not just for each other, but because God put you here for a reason.

Because we don't know it all, and we've still got a lot to learn, we decided to ask some of our friends what a relationship with God at the centre looks like for them.

Ian & Chris Francis

A relationship with God at the centre has meant everything. Especially because we weren't Christians for the first six years of our marriage - I guess we were 'us centred' and a bit selfish. Having God in the centre of 'us', our marriage, raising our family, our decisions, how we spend our time, our finances, the hard times, the happy times and everything else life brings, is everything. All we have is from Him and belongs to Him. We wouldn't want to live any other way.

Nick & Ella Brewer

A relationship with God at the centre has meant it is easier to forgive each other because we are both living in the reality of being forgiven, loved and accepted by Jesus.

Will & Claudia Adoasi

A relationship with God at the centre has meant that we have a foundation we both agree on and if we ever do not see eye to eye on an issue we go back to the foundation of love, forgiveness and hope. It helps us focus on what's important so we don't confuse the minor things for the major.

Our lives look different

When we come to know God for ourselves – receiving his grace, forgiveness, mercy that is new *every* morning, and the Holy Spirit to help us – our lives are bound to look different!

In Romans 12.2, we read 'Do not conform to the pattern of this world, but be transformed by the renewing of your mind. Then you will be able to test and approve what God's will is – his good, pleasing and perfect will.'

As Christ followers, understanding the truth about who God is and the truth of our identity in him renews the way we see ourselves and the world around us. Through this new understanding, we learn how to love others the way that we have been loved, and this can make us look so different to others in the world.

Jesus says in John 13.35, 'By this all people will know that you are my disciples, if you have love for one another.'

Let's say this prayer together:

God

I thank you that we can come to know you in a personal way and that you have made it possible for us to walk alongside you through our everyday lives. I thank you that you chose me before I chose you, and that you loved me before I even knew you. I pray that through this new understanding I can live a life of love for others that reflects more of who you are into the world.

Amen

An interview with

Griff

Griff has been singing, writing and producing her own music, since the age of ten. Now, age 19, she is signed to a major label, yet still sings in church most Sundays, unfazed by the world of fame and determined to walk with God every step of the way.

For Griff, God is her faithful friend who has seen her through family heartbreak, friendship drama, and given her a contagious confidence that made this interview SO much fun. Let's find out more...

Your life so far – what has it been like for you growing up?

I went to a normal mixed state school. I grew up in, and still live in, a tiny village called Kings Langley. But growing up, I always stuck out like a sore thumb; I was one of the only people of colour in my school and friendship groups – my Mum is Chinese, my Dad's Jamaican. I've got two older brothers, and then my mum fostered as well, so I have a big family!

You discovered your passion for music at quite an early age. Did people doubt you at first because you were so young?

Growing up in church, music is everywhere and so my passion for music probably started from going there and realizing I like the worship way more than I did the sermon! I started trying to write songs seriously when I was around ten. But people were very encouraging. I think that's because I was in a church community where everyone is so uplifting and wants to speak into your potential; I was definitely blessed in that sense. There was an element of 'child prodigy' around me though, with people saying things like 'oh my gosh, she's only ten and she can sing!' I used to hate my birthday, because I thought that maybe it lessened my talent if I was older. People say 'wow, she's 13 and she can hit that note', whereas it's less impressive when it's like 'oh she's 19 and...[Blank stare].' It's a weird complex in my head, but that was the way it was for me.

Did that make you put pressure on yourself to succeed at as young an age as possible?

Yeah, I think so. I'm very determined and go, go, go, and achieve now. I think I was a bit impatient with it, which is maybe a good or bad thing.

You said that your parents are from two different cultures. What was it like for you growing up in a multi-cultural household, whilst living in a really white area?

It was all I knew, but they're definitely two opposite cultures. Growing up with a mum who's not from here, there is definitely that culture difference between being a Western daughter and my mum obviously isn't. I think we're still learning how to navigate that. But yeah, it wasn't always rosy. I think I looked at the white, middle class family with a perfect mum and dad and kids with long blonde hair and thought that's really cool, but that's just not where I'm from. You know, I just kind of became used to it.

Did you feel like you had to embrace one side of your culture more than the other?

I kind of blocked out both in a sad way, and I think I've only just realized that when reflecting since

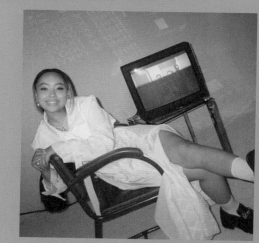

Black Lives Matter really erupted recently. The whole racism topic is weird anyway as a mixed-race kid, because you're kind of like I was never black enough to be black, never Chinese enough to be Chinese and definitely never white enough to be white. But I think I've realized upon reflection, I'd actually just cut off so much of being interested in both cultures because you just want to fit in and be like the other girls. I just wanted to be white, basically. Even to this day, I still straighten my hair because I think there is still a bit of a complex about what I see as 'fitting in' – it's so weird.

When listening to the lyrics of your songs, they sound like they come from a really real and authentic place. Do they come from your own personal experiences?

It's definitely personal, but with pop music, everyone always writes about love, and I never had a boyfriend and never experienced heartbreak so I was like, how do I even sing about that?

I definitely always try and find new things to sing about, and all the songs that sound like heartbreak, they're still real feelings, but just not a boy breaking my heart. Still, people have left my life, or I still trusted people that I wish I hadn't. Those kind of topics. I try and write openly so that everyone can relate to them.

A lot of people assumed that your song 'Good Stuff' was about a relationship heartbreak, but it wasn't, was it?

It was actually about how my family foster; kids come to live with us and they become like your brother and sister for years, and then they always move on. In that sense, every time you are getting your heart ripped out a little bit. Also, I feel like people don't share enough about friendship heartbreak. Being a teenage girl growing up, girls can be brutal. You can go through so many messed up friendship situations, and sometimes it really feels like heartbreak.

Do you think that seeing children with different life experiences come and go has helped you see the world through a different lens?

Yeah, I remember when we first started fostering and I was only eight, but I had a really romantic view of it. Watching Tracy Beaker was all I knew of kids in care so I was like – this is great, I get new siblings. And then they came and I remember the first kid started calling my mum, 'mum', and I was like, 'what the hell?' And then there was that whole revelation that you're really sharing your parents. I think it's definitely made me more independent and a little less selfish, I hope. I think it just made me get on with it, because my mum's now got new priorities. I've definitely learned from my mum seeing just how compassionate she is, and the supernatural love that it takes to love kids that aren't your own. It's easy to love your own kid, but when it's not your own blood, I think I've always been quite amazed at how easy she makes that look.

And hopefully I've taken on myself.

Did you grow up in church your whole life or did your family become Christians later on?

I was born and raised in church, going to a local church and then Hillsong when I was like thirteen. I think that was me going, OK, I do believe in this because I think when you're born and raised in church, you just go along with the motions until you reach that tension point in your teens when you're like, do I even care or believe in whatever my parents are telling me to believe in? Going to Hillsong definitely helped me figure out God for myself.

What do you think made you realize that you wanted to choose faith for yourself?

I think up until that point, there had been a lot of foundation building. Even though you're being told by parents to go to church, I still knew deep down that I couldn't deny who God is. I'd witnessed too much of God's grace on my family to completely not believe it, and I think it was more a thing of, 'you either dig deep or you don't.' Church became fun for me as well. It wasn't so much of a wrestle; it felt like it made sense at that point to choose church for myself.

You've had a personal relationship with God from quite a young age. How do you feel like you best relate to him?

I think it changes; the word 'season' is so Christian, but season to season it changes the way you see God. I think for me he's someone who's always there, ever-present. It's like wherever I go or whatever it is, if I'm doing all the smallest details of my life or making the biggest life decisions, God is always there.

You're actively involved with serving in church, but you also do a lot of stuff in the mainstream that isn't as directly related to being 'for church' or 'for God', so how do you allow your faith to

be a part of these things?

I think if you just believe in God and are trying to dig deeper and know God better in your private life, reading the Word and praying and asking God questions, then it's not so much 'I have to go out and preach the gospel' but an outpouring of who you are. I don't feel like 'oh no, I'm releasing a secular song, and I'm not doing things that are in church.' Like it's fine. Also through relationships and through conversation, people are intrigued about what it is I believe anyway.

If you could ask God one question, what would it be?

I'd probably ask him what Heaven's like. I try not to think about it too much because I don't know if it's something we can comprehend, and any time I try to, it will never justify what it's like. So yeah, I'd like to hear it from the horse's mouth - not that God's a horse!

Recently you did an interview and you styled and shot it all

yourself and made your own clothes. Is that true?

Yeah, I do it quite a lot. I took textiles in school and I just don't love that many clothes, or at least I've got things in my head that I want to wear. Stylists come in and they can be the best stylist ever and you can literally be wearing thousands of pounds worth of clothes, but it doesn't quite feel like you. So I just ended up making a lot of stuff and bringing it in to shoots because it just feels better.

What makes you so confident in being who you are or just being happy to be unique?

I think it probably stems from always sticking out when I was growing up. It's become something that I'm used to. You can choose to accept it or not, but the sooner you can accept it, it helps you out a little bit more in life. A lot of people do often say, 'you're confident!' or in the past they'd say, 'you're very mature for your age', and I don't really know what it is. I guess it is just a quality that for some reason

God's put in me. I like to think that allowed me to do what I'm doing now, and hopefully it will help me with whatever comes my way in the future. The truth is, though, I'm not always confident. We all have different sides of ourselves, and I have so many days where I'm completely indecisive and I have no idea whether things are good enough. With the job of putting out music, everything you do is public, so as confident as I am, I can also be very self-deprecating and pessimistic sometimes because you feel like everyone's always watching whether you succeed or fail.

There's a statistic that only around two per cent of music producers are female. Do you have any advice for girls that have dreams and aspirations to go into something that is currently a very male dominated industry?

I never overthought it. Producing my own music was a big selling point for me as a brand where everyone was like, 'she produces her own stuff'.

But it was never a thing where I set out to be a female producer. I think if there are things you love doing – just do it. I've realized that people really don't know what they're doing, or what they're talking about, and professionals really aren't that good. Everyone's just making it up, so just do it and have fun with it. And yeah, be confident with it. I think that's probably what helps me be confident when you realize that everyone's making it up anyway.

Is there any advice that you've ever received that has stuck with you?

It's such a generic thing to be like 'put God first,' and I think I always struggled with that because people always say that, and you're like, 'well, what does that even mean?' It's such an ambiguous thing to say. But over the years I've worked out that piece of advice; it means conscious conversation with God about everything you do. Even when you're feeling like you can't hear God, it's important to know God is in control.

Bible study 101

Where do I start?

Have you ever sat down to read your Bible, with a heart filled
with passion and desire to dig into God's word, but you have no
idea where to begin? We've all been there! So we've put together
a Bible Study 101 to help get you started.

Pray

Before you do anything, pray.

Pray that God will teach you something through what you're about to read and study and that you will hear his voice clearly. Pray against distractions and thank him for the provision of his Word.

Start

It doesn't matter where.

Yes, there are some easier books of the Bible to start in such as Proverbs or Psalms, but nowhere is there a bad start. Every part of the Bible has something for us – even the book of Numbers! You could choose a verse you have seen quoted somewhere, or one that you liked the sound of in church. Wherever you start, just start somewhere!

Context

This is important.

Don't just read one verse; read before and after it. This is to help you see who it was written by and why and where it was written. This is important because it adds substance to the verse(s) you're looking at. Always read more than one translation too, i.e. NIV, ESV, MSG. The variation of language will help broaden your understanding of what is being said.

Map it out & journal

It's time to dig a little deeper.

Highlight what stands out to you. Box any context (Who, Where, When). Circle words that you want to understand more fully. Write down any revelation or thoughts that you may have of what the text is saying to you.

Apply it

So what's next?

Take what you have read, studied and summarized and start to apply it to your life... is there something you should start doing, or stop doing? Or is it something you need to pray, think, talk or praise about?

Remember, God is always wanting to talk to us, to get closer to us, and one of his greatest ways of doing this is through his Word.

The
Girl Got Faith
glossary

There are words we will hear a lot in church and when reading the Bible, but we don't always know what they actually mean. Here's a glossary put together by our very own GGF theologian, Belle Tindall.

Salvation

Imagine you've fallen over and you're struggling to get back up, then suddenly you see a hand reaching out to help you to your feet again – that's a pretty good picture of salvation. It is being saved, being rescued, being picked back up by God. Salvation is knowing that God loves you and is holding you up, now (right here on earth) and forever (in heaven).

Repentance

Think of repentance as a U-turn. Salvation, mercy, grace, righteousness – they're all gifts that have very little to do with us and a whole lot to do with God; repentance, however, is a choice that is ours to make. We might notice that there is something specific in our lives that isn't good for us; maybe we're heading in a direction that isn't safe or healthy – and so we make a U-turn, we go a different way, we change our mind, we repent.

Holiness

We tend to hear that God is 'holy' a lot, don't we? This basically means that he is not like us, he's bigger, better and brighter than we could even imagine. Holiness is God rubbing off on us. The more we spend time with him, learn from him, do the things he does and say the things he says, the more we'll begin to look like Jesus. Obviously, we're not God, but we kind of are little pieces of him, little glimpses of his holiness. Pretty cool, huh?

Grace

If mercy wipes our messy slate clean, grace fills it back up with love. Grace is everything that we don't deserve but have anyway; we mess up and God adores us, we ignore him, and he sticks around, we run away and he chases us down. We can never earn grace; we could never even come close, and yet somehow, we're drenched in it.

Righteousness

God sees us as if we'd never once let him down. He keeps no record of the mistakes we make — that's pretty wonderful, right? God sees us through the lens of Jesus, and that right there, is righteousness.

Mercy

Whenever we mess up or disappoint ourselves, Jesus has got us utterly covered. He takes the blame for it all; he wipes our messy slates completely clean. And it's not just the things we've already done, but the mistakes we're sure to make in the future too. Mercy is our never-ending second chance.

Sin

The world we live in isn't perfect, is it? And nor are we. We don't have to look too far to notice that there are things in our world, in people we know and even in ourselves that seem unfair and very unlike Jesus, and that's sin. It is our messy, less- than- perfect selves, operating in a messy, less- than- perfect world.

Faithfulness

Faithfulness is the ability to stick around, to be present, to keep showing up. Faithful is something we always try to be, but it's also something God just is. He doesn't need to try; it's just part of his love for you. He'll always be there, he'll always come running, he'll never leave you or break one single promise. So, we match his faithfulness with our own (knowing that he'll always be way better at it than we are) and think of all the fun we'd miss if we left him hanging.

Joy

This one may seem pretty obvious, but we can actually get joy tangled up with feeling happy, and the two aren't always the same thing. Happiness is an emotion. It's something we feel. But joy is a choice we can make. It is choosing to delight in and celebrate the very fact that we are known, seen and loved by God. This means that joy can be found in the hardest of times; if God is around, joy is around.

Faith

Last but nowhere near least - faith is a gift from God, a gift that we can spend our lives growing, stretching and deepening. Faith isn't about having everything figured out; it is about knowing that we don't have to. It isn't about having all the answers; it is about knowing the one who does. Faith is the ability to be confident in things that we can't physically see with our eyes, to be sure of what doesn't make sense to us, to be certain that every word listed here is overwhelmingly and beautifully true.

What's your story?
By Yasmin Elizabeth

A testimony is a chance to share your own personal experience with God and his message of hope for the world.

When writing my testimony, at first, I was a bit nervous as I didn't want to get it wrong, but then I remembered I was just sharing my truth and my own personal story with God so far, so there wasn't anything to be nervous about. I swapped that nervousness for excitement because it's beyond exciting to think the same God who we read so many cool stories about in the Bible is the same God that we get to speak to and speak about daily.

Fill out the template opposite with your own story, and you'll have your very own testimony written out and ready to share!

Remember this is your truth and story. It's ok if it wasn't a smooth sailing one – mine certainly didn't include staying on the right path for very long at first – and equally it's ok if once you made your decision to follow Christ, that was it, boom, no looking back. Everybody's story is special and unique, just the way God made us, and he loves it when we talk and share the good news about him! Enjoy this process and have fun with it!

Watch Yasmin's testimony on Youtube:
Yasmin Elizabeth: **Testimony Time**

As I sat down with my notebook, I remembered first spending some time in prayer and then thinking about who I was before Jesus and how I came to know him.

Who were you and what was your life like before Jesus?

How did you first hear about Jesus? How did it make you feel?

When was the moment you knew you wanted to follow Jesus?

What challenges have you had to face in your faith?

What's life like now with Jesus?

Set your
minds on
things that
are above,

not on things that are on earth

Colossians 3:2
ESV

Contents

Looking ahead

You've made it through the last two sections, so hopefully you've discovered a few new things about who you really are, that your identity is something that can only be given to you by the one who created you – and it is unchanging! You may go through different phases of life, different hairstyles, schools or friendship groups, but the fact you are loved, chosen, and fearfully and wonderfully made does not and cannot change.

You will also have hopefully discovered more about God and how you can relate to him in a personal way. He isn't sitting up in the heavens, angry and judging your every move; he is closer than you think and looking on you with love, doing what he can to draw you closer to him, no matter what circumstance you are in.

These truths are foundational for how we live our lives. When we truly believe these things in our hearts, it can shape the way we dream about our future and what we believe is possible! So now is the time for us to look ahead and explore those beautiful dreams of yours and how, through you and the way you love people, the world might get to see and know more of who God is!

What's my purpose?

'What is my purpose?' has got to be up there with the top ten most-asked questions ever.

An old philosopher once said: 'He who has a why can endure any how.' We long to know our purpose because it enables us to focus, have clear direction and push forward, no matter what the obstacles may be.

However, we often end up mistaking purpose as being a specific job or lifestyle, and people spend years and lots of money travelling the world trying to discover their purpose. But the truth is we only have to open up our Bible to discover it.

Bring my sons from afar and my daughters from the ends of the earth—everyone who is called by my name, whom I created for my glory [emphasis added], whom I formed and made (Isaiah 43.6-7).

This one verse shares the secret – you were created for God's glory! If that's not purpose, then what is? God created all things for his glory; it is the great, overarching purpose for you and everything else!

Think back to the beginning of this book where we spoke about being made in God's image. This meant that the creation of us was a reflection of God, and everything down to our physical appearance can mirror something of him. So when it comes to our purpose, the things we choose to do, what we put our energy into, our 'mission', it makes sense that it is also to bring God glory.

Paul says in Philippians 1.20, 'with full courage now as always Christ will be honoured in my body, whether by life or by death.' This is a simple way for us to understand that living out our purpose means that in everything we do, all areas of life and even death, we can do it in a way that magnifies Jesus.

When we understand this truth, that we are already in the midst of our purpose, it unveils a whole new level to what you are able to do with your life. You see, your purpose doesn't need to be as specific as the career you choose or the country you live in, so don't sweat it. There isn't a one-way route through the course of your life. Instead, this releases us to know that we can live unique, exciting and adventurous lives that bring glory to God in a whole range of ways.

Hey again

I wanted to chip in with another thought on living and dreaming
faithfully with God.

When I was growing up, the things that formed my idea of how my
future would pan out were based on all the things I could see
around me. I assumed I would get married and have children because
that's what my parents had done, and I assumed I would find a 9–5
office job that I would do until I was 65, and then I'd retire and maybe
move to the seaside, because that's what my grandparents did.

The school system I grew up in was all about learning a range
of subjects but focusing on Maths, English and Science because they
were the basic qualification requirements for the office job I would
have in the future. I was never exposed to seeing a life where people did
exciting or unique careers, so I assumed that my life would follow that
same pattern.

I was limiting the dreams I could have for my life based on the things
I could see in front of me, and I was reaching only for what I knew was
already attainable in my own strength.

But as God graciously began dropping passion in my heart for what is now Girl Got Faith, I started to have vision for a life, career and a platform that I had never seen anywhere else. Through eyes of faith, I was able to put plans in place that meant I could work toward that vision even when it still seemed impossible based on my current circumstances.

I had a revelation that I didn't want to live a life where I do what is achievable in my own strength with a bit of hard work and determination. Instead, I want to live a life that is so far beyond my natural capability that I have no doubt in my mind that it is the strength of God alone that is making things happen. I want to live in partnership with God, and that means dreaming bigger than what I can physically see with my own eyes and asking God to impart his vision in me. And you can do the same.

I pray that as you begin or continue to journey with God, you wouldn't stress too much about what you can see or cannot see, but that you will rest in the knowledge that he has good plans for you. I believe in you – but he believes in you the most.

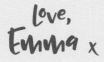

love,
Emma x

Something spectacular

By Lydia Mormen

For a long time I had one goal for my life, and that was to do something spectacular. I wasn't quite sure how it would look or what it would be, but I knew that I wanted my life to make an impact...

Growing up with social media makes it even easier to dream big. It's easy to dream about having the same lifestyle as our favourite singer, to analyse the career moves of someone that we admire or to keep updated with the amazing achievements of our friends.

But with so much access to other people's stories, it becomes really easy to lose sight of our own.

"Before I know it, I start to compare my own hopes and dreams with everyone else's. When I look at the place I am at on my imaginary 'success road map', compared with the people I admire, it can feel like I am way behind, and I feel disheartened. Doubts start to creep in about whether my 'something spectacular' really is that spectacular after all, and my enthusiasm dwindles as I start to think that maybe someone else could do it better.

Does this sound familiar? I am slowly learning that the reason this happens to so many of us is because our focus is in the wrong place. When we focus on ourselves and the spectacular things that we can achieve in our lives, it allows space for comparison to slowly creep in.

As daughters of God, we are invited to turn our gaze away from worrying about how spectacular we are and to focus on how spectacular he is. He becomes the main character in our story, which takes the pressure off of us.

When we begin to change our focus from the pressure of doing something spectacular in our own strength to simply abiding in his, we begin to realize that his plans for our lives were more spectacular than anything we could have done on our own. It eliminates the problem of comparison because we are no longer living to glorify ourselves, and we can focus on using the gifts he has given us to glorify him instead.

I am so encouraged when I look at the Bible and the lives of the disciples. Out of everyone in Israel, Jesus chose 12 men, who led very normal, unspectacular lives, and made them into God-glorifying world-changers. There was no IQ test or popularity contest that they had to complete first; he didn't choose the 12 that had the best business plan—all they had to do was say yes to one simple instruction: 'Follow me.'

These men weren't seeking to lead spectacular lives; some of them even went back to their old jobs before they knew Jesus had been resurrected! All they knew was that they had encountered a spectacular God and wanted to follow him and his plans, wherever that took them.

God doesn't promise that when we follow him and choose his plan over our own that it will look exactly like we imagined, but the Bible does tell us this:

God can do anything, you know – far more than you could ever imagine or guess or request in your wildest dreams! He does it not by pushing us around but by working within us, his Spirit deeply and gently within us (Ephesians 3.20).

I don't know about you, but that sounds pretty spectacular to me.

God can do anything, you know — far more than you could ever imagine or guess or request in your wildest dreams!

Ephesians 3:20

Do you know you are already enough? Read that again: you're already ENOUGH.

Even if you never do anything else for the rest of your life, you are enough. Culture today can be all too quick to glorify the stuff that we do, produce and achieve, rather than who God has made us to be. And yet, once we fully grasp this truth – that we are qualified by God and God alone – then this becomes the perfect foundation from which to dream with God.

What do you imagine is possible for you to do in life? Now think of the impossible; think of things that feel so out of reach that you could never get there on your own – it would take the miraculous. THAT'S what life is like with God. The dreams God has for us may look 'big' in the world's eyes – like becoming an actor like Letitia Wright or a singer like Griff – or they may look relatively 'small' to the world, like befriending your neighbour or journeying with one person in their faith. But when it comes to dreaming with God, all dreams are big dreams.

When we only do the things that are possible in our own strength, we are not living with faith in God; we are living with faith in ourselves. If Ephesians 3.20 is really true, and God really can do anything, far more than I could ever imagine, why settle for less? There's a whole future of excitement, adventure and challenge just waiting for you – if only you would put your trust in the one who will make it happen.

Life lessons with

Naomi Scott

A multi-talented actress, singer, songwriter, director and producer, (pauses for breath), Naomi Scott is not only the best friend we wish we all had, but the embodiment of a modern artist who refuses to be pinned down.

Although more recently known for her role as Jasmine in Disney's live-action remake of Aladdin, she has none of the supposed pretension. Despite the glitz and glamour of Hollywood, it's her faith which is the foundation of every decision she makes and has been the grounding force throughout her life and career so far.

The daughter of a British-Indian mother and a white British pastor father, she was born in Hounslow and moved to Woodford, Essex, in her teens. At school, Naomi was a self-confessed 'floater', never entirely fitting the mould when it came to friendship groups or expectations. It was only when she was around music and drama that she felt like she had truly found her place.

It was actually in her dad's church – the one she still attends today – at the age of 15, that she was first spotted by an agent who signed her after hearing her sing Alicia Keys at a talent show. From that moment, Naomi threw herself into auditions and landed her first role in a Disney show, *Life Bites*, which she filmed while sitting her GCSE's, then going on to film *Lemonade Mouth*, and later skipping her A Levels for a main role in Steven Spielberg's' *Terra Nova*. Amidst all of the auditions and travel, Naomi also managed to fit in marrying her husband, Jordan Spence, when she turned 21,

whom she met through church around the same time as getting spotted.

Safe to say, Naomi isn't the classic 'English rose' we used to send to Hollywood, and this is something she's spoken about at length.

Being British-Indian, her multiracial background has often proven confusing for Hollywood.

'I was the nearly girl for a long time,' she recounts. Auditioning for numerous roles, only to be told she wasn't quite what they had in mind, became a familiar thing, '[I was] too white for some roles, and too 'not-white' for others'.

But rather than allow this colour-casting debate to deter her, she has in fact turned what was an obstacle into an opportunity, launching New Name Entertainment in 2020 alongside her husband – a production company primarily concerned with

the prioritizing of diversity in both narrative and talent – seeking out the stories that have long gone untold.

Charismatic, talented, and refreshingly down to earth, Naomi speaks so much wisdom into a culture that is obsessed with a prescriptive portrayal of female perfection. She's been a Disney Princess and has serious eczema; she can belt out an orchestral ballad, and yet loves to stank face to Kirk Franklin (Love Theory – check it) in her trackies; she loves her mum's dahl and would also happily polish off a roast.

She couldn't be anyone else if she tried, so she doesn't.

Small examples which illustrate the way in which she is setting the brilliant example of embracing the fullness of who you are – and arguably, that is what true success looks like.

As a long standing friend of Girl Got Faith, there from the very beginning, we asked if Naomi would share her top ten life lessons that she's picked up along the way. Take note, girls, you're going to want to remember these!

10 *Life Lessons:*

01. Keep the main thing the main thing. My husband often reminds me of this. In other words, sometimes it's sooo easy to slowly veer away from what really matters, to forget why we do what we do, or whom we serve. Daily reminding myself of the things which truly matter really helps to determine those small everyday choices I make.

02. If you've grown up in church, you'll know the phrase 'Well...God's still on the throne'. Quite honestly, I used to think to myself...well isn't that an easy way to palm off the evil in the world? But it wasn't until I was

in a dark place, that the truth of that statement was actually the strength that got me through.

It doesn't mean things aren't hard and don't hurt, but it does mean that the scariest things that happen to us don't scare God, that he isn't some panicked human. He is with you through it and ultimately in control of everything. Phew.

03. Listen

04. Look at the people you spend the most time with...you are them. If that's not who you wanna be then consider who you prioritize your time with.

05. Trying to understand others through our personal experience alone never works.

06. Never wear black tights with open toe beige shoes.

07. Failure isn't something to be terrified of. I've often felt that I fail over and over again; it was something constantly on my mind. But then one day, I realized that if I treat every day like a new day, even though I may still 'fail' loads, the pressure is off, and I find myself keeping up certain good habits.

08. Don't read the comments...ever.

09. In a work environment, being fully prepared allows you to be assertive about what you need in order to do your job well. People will usually match that energy and respect your work ethic.

10. Ask yourself the question, 'What is success to me?' It's easy to subtly start making decisions in your own life based on what someone else's idea of success is.

Dream, then do

Did you know that vividly describing your dreams and goals in written form is strongly associated with achieving them? People who very vividly describe or picture their goals are anywhere from 1.2 to 1.4 times more likely to successfully accomplish their goals than people who don't.

So, we are going to make a start on getting these wonderful dreams of yours onto paper, and then we'll work together on some practical things you might need to do to start seeing them happen!

When you're dreaming
big and discovering what could
be possible with your life,
consider some of the following...

What is a need that you have noticed in the world,
or something that you feel passionate about?

What comes naturally to you that might seem difficult,
or overwhelming, for others?

When you imagine your best life
ten years from now, what do you see?

You've got the dreams, but now you need a plan. Answer the following questions to help to give your ideas the next practical steps...

If you were to take one step in building your future this week, what one thing could you do?

Write down a scripture that encourages
you to be the best that you can be and stick
this somewhere you will see it every day.

Who inspires you? Does he or she have any content
you can read online or if it is someone in your life, can you
arrange to spend an afternoon with this person?

Parable of the talents

In the New Testament, there are some mini-stories that Jesus uses to illustrate a teaching he is trying to share; these are called 'parables'. There are quite a few different ones, but the one we are going to look at is found in Matthew 24.14–30, the parable of the talents.

Jesus tells a story about a master who was going away on a journey and left 'talents', i.e. money, with his three servants, who each had to decide what to do with this money that was entrusted to them – with the knowledge that one day, when the master comes back, they will have to say what they did with it. Each of the servants was given a different amount and did different things with what he was given.

The Bible says that the master returned after a long time, which probably would have left the servants wondering if he would really ever return. But he did, and then it was time for them to present to the master the result of their stewardship.

The first two servants both 'put their money to work' and were able to double what was entrusted to them and gave that to the master on his return. He was very pleased and said 'Well done, good and faithful servant! You have been faithful with a few things; I will put you in charge of many things. Come and share your master's happiness!' (Matthew 24.19, 23). However, the third servant was afraid of the master and decided to simply bury the money in the ground until he returned so that he could give him back exactly what was given to him. The master was very unhappy about this and called him a 'wicked and lazy servant!' (Matthew 24.26).

Remember, when Jesus tells these stories, he is actually trying to teach us something important to apply to our own lives.

The first lesson is that everything we have is given to us by God; it is entrusted to us for this life here on earth, but one day we will have to account for what we did with what we were given. Some may interpret this to be just about money, but we believe it can be about anything you have in your life, including your gifts and talents!

The second lesson is that the same way each of the servants was given a different amount, so are we! We can spend too much time being envious of others or complain that we don't have as much as someone else, but the point is that it isn't about how much you have, but what you do with what it is. We must take responsibility for what has been given to us, no matter how much little.

The third lesson is that our view of God is important and affects the way we live our lives. If we view God as a harsh ruler with unfair expectations of us, we will end up treating what has been given to us like the third servant – with fear and unprofitable results. However, if we understand that God actually wants to bless us, and wants us to share in his happiness, then we will use the gifts he has given us with so much more freedom, knowing that what he has given us does not ultimately belong to us that we can be confident that we were entrusted with whatever we have for a reason and we have the ability to manage it well and see fruitfulness from it.

What gifts, talents, or even material possessions have you been entrusted with, and how can you use them with freedom and confidence that will ultimately bring glory back to the one who gave you everything?

Generation to generation:

"Let this be recorded for a generation to come, so that a people yet to be created may praise the Lord" – Psalm 102:18

When we think of our dreams and our do's, it's important to remember that our lives are meaningful but also just a speck in light of eternity. This thought shouldn't make you shrink back or think, 'what's the point?' but instead empower you to think about the part you are playing in the world beyond your years here on earth.

Throughout the Bible, we see times when God has started a 'project' with someone, but the completion came after they had passed away and it was someone else who got to see the conclusion. Like Moses who led the Israelites out of slavery in Egypt and wandered the desert for many years, but never set foot in the promised land. It was his successor, Joshua who got to complete the task of bringing the Israelites into the promised land. You can read more about this in the book of Exodus.

Or how about King David who had it on his heart to build a temple to be used to worship God. God even gave David all of the plans, the vision, everything – but God said it would not be David who got to build it, but instead his son Solomon who would. And David, though he must have been a bit sad about this, understood that God's plan for humanity is so much bigger than our individual lifespans (1 Chronicles 28).

There is so much joy to be found when we can view our lives and the part we play in the grander scheme. It relieves the pressure that we must do it all right here, right now, and we can instead focus on seeking God and his plans and his ways and partnering with him to do what truly will bring us satisfaction and him glory.

I wonder what dreams you have that when put into action could shape the future generations that come after you.

Are you forging a path for someone else to follow you? Are you seeking to put in the often hard and uncomfortable work to break ceilings and barriers now that will provide opportunity for others?

Whom do you hope to impact?

Are there people in your life that you hope to impact? Can you begin by
praying for them? Whether there are individuals, a people-group,
a company or a whole country, write the names down here and make
this your commitment to pray for them and their needs.

Pay it forward

When we know who we are, whose we are and why we are here,
we naturally begin to live more outward-facing lives. We look for people
with whom to share the good news of Jesus, and we long to encourage
others with the same truth that we have come to realize for ourselves.
You've made it to the end of the book, so now is your time to pay
it forward.

*The page opposite is one you can use to write a letter of
encouragement to someone in your life.*

Although the journey of this book is now finished, the adventures of
your life with God are already waiting to happen! We are so excited
for you to step into your future with full knowledge of your identity as
a daughter, chosen, loved and accepted. It's exciting that you can walk
each day with God by your side, talking to him and involving him – and,
through this, you might discover dreams that have been placed on
your heart for how you can impact the world around you with all of the
wonder and greatness you carry.

About Girl Got Faith

Girl Got Faith believes that leading a faith-filled life doesn't have to be boring or full of rules, but it is something that can completely change your life for the better as you enjoy everything that God has in store for you. No matter if it's beauty, fashion, lifestyle, or faith, God cares about it just as much as you do, because He cares about you!

Whether it's online via our website or Youtube, or offline at one of our school workshops or events, Girl Got Faith hopes to raise fearless women of God that will influence and lead their generation.

girlgotfaith.com

@girlgotfaith

About Emma Borquaye

Emma is the founding editor of Girl Got Faith.
She started GGF back in 2015 when she realized there was a
lack of online resources for teenage girls who have questions
about life and faith. Over the last few years Emma has taken
GGF from an online blog, to developing a schools programme,
starting the YouTube channel, growing a dedicated social media
following, and spreading the GGF message through speaking
engagements. Emma lives with her husband and son in South
East London, and her greatest passion is to see young people
realize their full potential and find their confidence in who
God created them to be.

NOTES

A space to create

A space to create

Acknowledgements

When Girl Got Faith launched in 2015, it was my goal to see it have more followers than I do on Instagram so that I knew it wasn't just my friends and family being nice, but that it was actually reaching the girls whom it was intended. And then you came along...in your thousands! This book is for you, and it certainly wouldn't be possible without you. Thank you for the support over all these years and for trusting Girl Got Faith to play a small part in this beautiful journey of faith you are on.

Like everything Girl Got Faith does, it is always a collective effort, so a huge thank you to our publisher, SPCK, and everyone that has contributed their time and words to this book: Letitia, Griff, Naomi, Cheryl, Ashley, Yasmin, Lydia, Belle, Megan, Samantha, Isaac, Will, Claudia, Ella, Nick, and my very own Mum and Dad! Also to our incredible photographer Abbie, and the wonderful models Rachel, Tish, Izzy, Becca, Megan and Beth who all share the same heart for what we do.

A very special thank you to our designer Kate, who pulls everything together so beautifully - and to our editor Elizabeth who has so graciously walked us through every step of the way.

The final and most special thank you had to be reserved for God! This book is full of YOUR words, for YOUR daughters, and I am amazed when I consider the fact that you trusted Girl Got Faith to take care of this on your behalf.